HOTEL AT THE END OF THE WORLD

New Women's Voices Series, No. 161

poems by

Dinah Berland

Finishing Line Press
Georgetown, Kentucky

HOTEL AT THE END OF THE WORLD

New Women's Voices Series, No. 161

Copyright © 2021 by Dinah Berland
ISBN 978-1-64662-659-5 First Edition
All rights reserved under International and Pan-American Copyright Conventions.
No part of this book may be reproduced in any manner whatsoever without written
permission from the publisher, except in the case of brief quotations embodied in
critical articles and reviews.

Publisher: Leah Huete de Maines
Editor: Christen Kincaid
Cover Art: Terry Braunstein
Author Photo: Mehrnaz Davoudi
Cover Design: Elizabeth Maines McCleavy

Order online: www.finishinglinepress.com
also available on amazon.com

Author inquiries and mail orders:
Finishing Line Press
PO Box 1626
Georgetown, Kentucky 40324
USA

Table of Contents

Wild Bird Elegy 1
Blazon 2
Girl Waiting 3
Portrait, Age Seven 4
Dark Child 5
Sephirot 6
Ghazal for My Ancestors 8
The Invention of Singing 9
Line Dancing, 1960 10
At La Capilla 11
Not to Meet Beautiful Strangers 12
What Some Men Can Do 13
Blowfish 14
Blue Carnation 16
Last Judgment 17
A Walk at Dusk 19
Milk Glass 20
Reflections 21
Sonnet for Sarah 22
Five Years 23
Angeline 24
Running Away 25
From the 22nd Floor 26
El Norte 27
In a Strange Land 29
Pandemic Dog Walk 30
Tranquil Weather 31
Hotel at the End of the World 32

In memory of my parents and grandparents

*And for my children—Adam, Jessica, and Rebecca;
and my grandchildren, Hani and Mia*

Wild Bird Elegy
In Memory of Brigit Pegeen Kelly (1951–2016)

Spotting the torn book on the floor,
I scooped up my copy of *Song*

with a gasp—seeing the jagged gashes
through your impeccably crafted lines.

My finicky puppy picked out the book,
as was her fancy now that she was big enough

to pluck it from the shelf with her needle-sharp
teeth, as if to say, *This is what you need to read!*

But first she had to bite the spine and taste
the glue, ripping through the back cover

with its sepia-tone portrait of you,
scratching the ear of your biddable hound.

She couldn't know you had left us
only weeks before—bereft of all

the songs that might still have come
from your singular voice. Then I saw

your inscription penned to me in long,
loping strokes—saw the "wild bird" dive

straight from your hand to my ribcage,
where it flutters and beats—
beats and flutters still.

Blazon

My mother with her long, dangly earrings
With her elephant-ear sponges and magnifying mirrors
With her dusty catalogs in boxes
With her fashion magazines
With her sable-hair brushes
With nudes and trumpets in her trompe l'oeil paintings
With her portraits of me at all ages
My mother with her mink jacket and lipstick kisses
With her cigarette holder and beehive hairdo
With her dressmaker's dummy
With her boutique charge accounts
My mother who designed pinafores and submarine insignia
With her plunging necklines and Florida tan
With her party games and piano music
With her lucky queen of hearts laughter
My mother who sang "Nature Boy" and cried
With her fear of strangers, chills, and natural disasters
My mother who amazed her doctors for sixteen years
And said her last words, "She did a good job,"
When I held up her painting of a ballerina in the clouds
My mother who insisted I keep her age a secret, even
On her headstone, and hated her face
In the mirror at the hospice
A mask of wax stretched across her cheekbones
With her breathing like a freight train, like a feather
With her hand turning blue as it clutched mine
My mother with her paintings of brilliant birds
With her secret life as a dancer

Girl Waiting

One dark braid down the middle of my back,
pigeon feather in my pocket,
I smoothed out my blanket in the thicket
over leaves that smelled of walnut bread
and rain. I sat cross-legged there, under
a canopy of brambles, listening
for footsteps, listening for drums.
I was safe inside the thicket, invisible
as I drew stick pictures in the sand.
Looking up through a clearing in the canopy,
I read signals in the clouds. I was sure
if I waited long enough
my true mother would come
and pluck me from the thicket.
She wouldn't hold me to the mirror
and tell me how ugly I looked when I cried,
wouldn't twist my legs into pretzels
and pretend to eat me up. She wouldn't
wear high heels, tight dresses, or lipstick.
She would be big, with a soft lap, and quiet,
her hair dark and shiny like mine.
She would know I was her daughter
as soon as she saw me, take me
home, feed me corncakes
and tell me all the stories
I had been waiting to hear.

Portrait, Age Seven

It's not the wave
that will devour you,
arms and braids and all.
Not even the stranger
you won't look at
in the shiny car. Not
the topography of deserts,
where you follow streambeds
through the night, gobbling up
the stars like sugar,
ready to break
the moon in half.

Not even the mountain that turns
to day-old bread beneath your feet
or sends hot lava
to your door. You can always
take the brittle
sticks that thrash you
and bind them into rafts to
carry you downriver. Listen
to the winter trees.
They will teach you
about emptiness.

And one more thing: although
you may be brave—don't go
with that sweet honeysuckle man,
the one who wants to
scoop you up
on his ice-cold steed and burn
your thighs. His captain's cap
is made of smoke and acid. He is
the father of your children. He will
eat them all alive.

Dark Child

Salvadoran soccer players kick a checkered ball
across South Central grass, their red and purple socks
flashing past chain link until the forward knocks
the ball into the goal—close call for Los Rojos,
victors in this pocket park at dusk
with sirens and dogs wailing in shrill dissonance,
the scent of kerosene rising from a grill
the way it did when you were a kid and knew
the night streets were forbidden, as you watched the sky
ripen and bleed like the stain of a red-hearted plum,
longing to mount your three-speed bike—fly
over suburban curbs toward the thrum
of the city, singing a foreign song until
no one could tell where you belonged.

Sephirot

He was eighty-one years old when he drew the letters
in my tablet. I remember how he moved
the pencil slowly as he wrote my name
in letters that added up to numbers
the way he learned them in the village near Odessa
when he was a boy, before he was my Grandpa.

I traced the dotted pictures Grandpa
made: teapots, black-hat and candelabra letters.
Girls, even at thirteen, were not taught Kabbalah in Odessa.
But *This is a free country*—so he showed me how he moved
the *aleph, mem,* and *shin* to make a riddle out of numbers
and I knew it was as important as my name.

Sarah Bat Avram Yakov was my name.
When I was called to the Torah, Grandpa
closed his eyes. He was reciting Hebrew numbers,
turning them to songs with backward letters,
rocking back and forth as he moved.
He was so far from Jerusalem, so very far from Odessa.

Why did he and Grandma leave their home in Odessa?
When I asked him this, I could not name
the strange look on his face. Some said they moved
because Lake Michigan resembled the Black Sea. Grandpa
played cards in the park. Grandma wrote letters
and gazed across the water. What number

of people? How many boats? They must have numbered
in the thousands—Jews who called Odessa
home for generations, fleeing the pogroms. Letters
clipped to our family tree told the story later, gave a name
to the horror, explained why Grandma and Grandpa
picked up their infant daughter and moved

with one small diamond sewn inside a coat. They moved
like leaves on water, swept up in endless numbers
of émigrés to Ellis Island. This is how it happened: Grandpa
heard his wife scream as she ran from the market in Odessa.
She had seen the Cossacks grab a pregnant woman and—in the name
of the czar—cut her open, stuff her abdomen with straw. *Some letters
have no sound.* They moved like air, like fire, like water, with letters
that spelled the unspeakable name of God in numbers:
Grandpa Isaac, his wife Paula, and their daughter from Odessa.

Ghazal for My Ancestors

I'm on a double-helix rollback toward my ancestors,
An unfurled scroll reaching back to my ancestors.

My skin cells replace themselves every seven years.
Time is a great healer is the feedback from my ancestors.

The fiddler's fingers move so fast they disappear.
This is no time to attack my ancestors.

In history class we learn about wars
But not about the Cossacks and my ancestors.

The old wall in Jerusalem is dotted with prayers.
I tuck a prayer between the stones for my ancestors.

The lowest note (B-flat) was just discovered emanating
From a black hole. Is that the black coat of my ancestors?

I stay up late, singing songs to the stars.
I must be an insomniac like my ancestors.

This teacup might topple or burst into flame.
Anything is possible if I take the tack of my ancestors.

I paint my study terracotta to let joy enter.
When I let joy enter, I'm on the right track to my ancestors.

One day may the little fiddler girl lie down in Ein Gedi
Under a river of stars, the rising sign of my ancestors.

The Invention of Singing

Maybe it emanated from the solar wind
before there was a sun. Maybe each of us arrives
with a portion of the melody, like last night
in the backyard tent, where we gathered
under palm fronds and strings of tiny lights
for the festival of Sukkot. We savored
couscous, stuffed grape leaves, yogurt
with mint, drank wine and told stories
into the cool blue evening at the long table,
when all at once a barrel-chested man
began to clap and chant a wordless tune
that caused us to become like braided
bread, some climbing up and over,
some humming in the middle
until we had switched places. It was
the joining that we loved. We sang
in gratitude for surviving to this day
not too badly wounded, our firstborn sons
not wrenched from our arms—not this time,
none of us stoned to death with rock-
hard fruit for some obscure transgression.
We had reason to sing *hi-la-lai la-lai
la-la-lai,* a song of hallelujah.
Maybe it was this simple: the notes,
some loud, some soft, some held in the mouth
like a secret, drifted up with candle smoke
to the Eternal Singer, who was circulating
through the tent at that very moment, lighting fires
in the firmament behind our eyes, pulsing
through our corpuscles, breathing
through our lungs, our throats,
our vocal chords, using our very bodies
to invent the art of singing.

Line Dancing, 1960

I'm outside of town tonight—
a dark-skinned Jewish girl, line
dancing in a shack after midnight.

My freckled, ginger-haired date
wants to know if I took him for
white when we met. I ask him

if he thought I was Black. We
line dance along the edges, erasing
lines of demarcation as the music

takes us down—*a'right, a'right!*
Step left and turn, brush right—
I used to wonder why

we never touched when we lay
side-by-side on the narrow bed
that afternoon, sun spilling

through the linen curtain—
don't even remember his last name,
but I've never forgotten how it felt

to breathe in sync with him—
like sipping sunlight from the sky.
Haven't forgotten Ray Charles either,

his smoky voice sailing through the air
as we slid left and right across
the dimly lit room into the night—

line dancing to the rhythm,
line dancing to the beat—*you
got it now, girl—a'right, a'right.*

At La Capilla

My mother joined us for dinner last night,
though she's been dead fourteen years.
She couldn't help herself. She saw the heavy
pewter platters, white napkins folded
into bishops' hats, the staccato lights
rat-a-tat-tatting across the verandah
below the pink stone church.
She was lured by the Latin waiter
as he brushed past my shoulder to slide
a bowl of tomato bisque onto my plate,
his crisp linen jacket, his transparent aura.
She saw you sitting there
with your mind elsewhere,
and she had to rush over to say,
*Wait a minute. Aren't you forgetting
something? I'd be flirting with that waiter
right now if he could see me—
and with your husband, too. He's quite
a cutie, you know. Hang on to him!*
Does she know something I don't?
If I ignore her, maybe she'll vanish
into the clouds amassing behind
the pink church dome and I can
disregard her warning. Maybe
she'll slip into that gyrating light
those waiters are pointing to right now,
whispering something in Spanish ¿en el cielo?
pointing and staring, as your top-ten
bonbons, muses, gun molls, sirens—
all dressed in strapless evening gowns,
glide down a celestial escalator
and head straight over to our table.

Not to Meet Beautiful Strangers

Not to stay in pink stucco hotels with
Venezuelan maids to shake sand out of your sheets
or to pitch tent on Secret Beach under
satinwood trees with a woman half your age.

Not to burst red caviar on your tongue at breakfast,
drink calvados until your arms catch fire
or walk from brothel to museum to see how
Picasso shattered his wives.

Not to sink to the top of your waders in the stream,
casting to a pool beneath the willows
or sip beer at sunset with beautiful strangers,
waiting for your island flight.

Not even to ride horseback across Africa,
where Bedouin women gave you chickens
for removing bracelets of worms
that spiraled up their children's ankles.

Not to be sentenced to house arrest—
Is that why you always travel light? *I'm not
a bloody oak,* you sigh, your cigar smoke
rising to the ceiling one breath ahead of your body.

What Some Men Can Do

Your friend Nash stands at the intersection
of streets made out of water, casting his line
from the curb. He doesn't have to wait;
an enormous trout rises to the surface
and swallows his hand-tied ginger quill.

The fish is much too big to bring in
with his number two line, so Nash dives in
headfirst, and with the strength reserved
for dreams, yanks the speckled thing
out of the water. Thrusting his arm
down to the elbow into the trout's jaws,
he pulls out a smaller fish
the bigger one has swallowed. *Just look
at this mother!* he shouts.

I stand at the curb, amazed
by what some men can do, recalling
the time my first husband jumped off
the tour boat in Naples Harbor,
too impatient to wait for docking.

Like him, you dive in after Nash, your
T-shirt—the one with the rainbow trout
swimming from armpit to armpit
—billows like a sail tacking
into the wind, your body sending
splashes up the sidewalk
like cryptic farewell notes.

Blowfish

Driving with the X-ray—a shadow
of something abnormal in it—

tucked inside my briefcase,
my mouth tastes metallic, as if

I'd eaten a delectable morsel
of blowfish, the kind of sushi

that can kill you. The terror
is so palpable I am lifted

out of my car like a spiny puffer
drifting through the ocean

right here in the city, where
everyone is doing what needs

to be done: unloading boxes,
walking the dog, stepping

off the curb when the light
turns green—their gestures

so rhythmic, so graceful, I long
to be one of them forever. Instead

I'm watching a film in which
couples dance on the deck of a ship

while in the bird's eye view
you can see the collision coming.

The air is a luminous blue, dark
and bright at once, the color

of an iceberg in moonlight,
the same shape as my right breast—

the one with the 7-mm nodule
lodged inside it like a bullet.

I feel a riptide pulling my body
out to sea, and all I can do is keep driving.

Blue Carnation
Elegy for William Bowman

Is that you on the bar stool, nibbling
fromage, wearing a blue carnation
in the lapel of your rumpled jacket?
How I want it to be you, twirling
your tequila glass with those artistic fingers,
about to tell a stranger how you sold your house
in Silver Lake and bought a Duchamp box,
only to be hounded by the IRS for years,
how you moved to Arles to make art
but couldn't make yourself young again.
I can almost make myself believe it is you,
though all I can see from this angle
is the shock of dun-colored hair
across your brow and enough of your
angular profile to imagine
that you didn't die in your car
in a field in Provence, surrounded
by Van Gogh's crows, garden hose
jammed from exhaust pipe
to window crack—didn't die because
I saw you just in time, your straight hair
falling across your brow the way it does now,
your hands resting against the steering wheel
as if you were holding me by the shoulders—
saw you just in time to run full throttle
through waist-high weeds as if in a dream
I could not change, with eager burrs
grabbing my skirt, field stones knocking me
off balance until I fell in a descent
so melodramatically Dada, stumbled
downhill toward the door to your car
just in time to see the blue carnation blooming
at your brow and know I was too late,
too late to change the story
you must have known that I would tell.

Last Judgment
> *One feeling alone reigns, that of violent terror.* —E. Ollivier, 1892

He never wanted to paint it,
being a man of marble, but when
the second pope insisted, he lumbered
up the scaffold to face the altar wall.
From lapis lazuli and ochre, from marble dust
and verdigris, he made men and women,
released bone and sinew from the skin
of damp plaster, twisted and turned them
until their bodies tumbled, weightless,
writhing in confusion.

Every face became a face of grief
or terror—not only the misery
of sinners tripping over one another
as they fell, helpless, toward the dark river
or the bewilderment of the resurrected dead
wrenched from restless sleep but also
the misery of the saved: weightless virgins
unable to refuse their own ascension,
St. Peter pleading, despite the key to Paradise
shining in his hand—all the blessed
and the damned caught up in one great
swirl of souls so wretched even the angels
could not grant them courage.

In the center, he made Jesus
conductor of the storm, arm raised
in mid-gesture, a split-instant before
the final trumpet blast—yet nude as all the rest:
his chiseled nose and high cheekbones as classic
as Apollo's. *There are a thousand heresies,*
the critics cried, pointing *to the man being dragged down
by his genital members, that even the brothel
would shut its eyes in order not to see it.*

But the painter was not done. He saved
the coup de grace for the pope's auxiliary,
Biago da Cesena, who demanded
loincloths be painted over every *obscenity*.
On the ass-eared Minos, demon at the lowest gate,
he put the critic's likeness—boa constrictor
coiled around his torso, asp snapping
at his tiny member. When Biago
protested to the pope, the Holy Father replied,
If it were Purgatory, I could help you,
but I have no authority in Hell.

Finally, on the flayed hide draped across
the arm of the martyred St. Bartholomew,
the master placed his own self-portrait, freed
from the skull's marble armature, splattering
red pigment into the River Styx.

A Walk at Dusk
After a painting by Caspar David Friedrich (1774–1840)

Come with me, toward the leafless trees. See
the way they lean, dazed with fog and grief
as they seek out one another in the haze?
Isn't that how we are able to go on—by believing
all that matters will one day be revealed?
That is why I made the waxing moon so sharp,
its violet face aglow, why I put the moon under
the influence of Venus, though we know
these lovers are light years from each other.
But I have not brought you here to talk about
astronomy or painterly technique but rather
magnetism of a different order. Over there—
now you see it: the megalithic tomb.
See how that massive rock appears to float
like a ship asunder? This weighty sepulcher
will not leave me alone. I have painted it
under a hood of snow, girdled it in broken oaks,
glazed it with opaque aspersions. Some evenings,
walking here alone, I am that rock—or I am
a man trapped beneath its lid, dense
with melancholia, my fur hat a granite wheel,
my stained hands sunk deep into the pockets
of my cape. I have heard it said that memory
is a form of recovery, a healing. But sometimes
when I venture to this field at the dislocating
hour—the very hour that slips across
our foreheads at this moment, before
the earth rolls over in the star-cast void
like a capsized ship and all of us gone with it—
memory breaches the grave. Walk with me
a while, I pray you. I am drowning on dry land,
and only a stranger's gaze can save me.

Milk Glass

My bathroom mirror is a window
with a sash I could throw open
if it were not painted shut.
Above it hangs a transparent pane
high enough to frame the sky.
Usually I forget this, as in the evening
while putting on my makeup
I am surprised by a streak of orange
or zigzag of dark wings headed for the sea.

Stepping from the shower, I see nothing
but vapor in the mirror
and in the square above, no telling
the difference between cloud
and condensation. I am nowhere
in this picture and everywhere at once,
the way the blind woman said she sees—
as if her face were pressed against milk glass.

This glass of misted silver breaks
my face apart, scatters all its light
the way the soul goes when it flies
out of the body, or music as it leaves
the tip of the conductor's baton
to begin its endless journey into space
where no one will ever say:
This was *The Swan of Tuonela*
by Sibelius who died at 92. This was
his cliff of cellos rising with vibrato
from the orchestra of death, beating
at his dark and rain-streaked window.

Reflections
For Adam

In the mirror mounted on the ceiling,
I saw your hand first. You were born that way,
waving, about to embark into a world of air,
for I could no longer carry you in water—
waving good-bye and hello at once, arm
overhead, fingers outstretched, reaching
for something of substance to hold.
Now, face to face at the airport gate, after
eighteen years of holding tight
and letting go, you carry my reflection
in your eyes back to the Great Lakes,
where I was born. I watch you walk onto
the airfield. Just before you step onto the staircase,
you turn around and, in slow motion, like a child
born hand first, burst into the world
alone, waving—you wave to me again.
I wave back and wish I could toss you a line, a raft,
a talisman—something more solid than reflection,
something of substance to hold.

Sonnet for Sarah

My son, Isaac, is from paradise.
He does everything his father tells him.
Today they set out to make a sacrifice
on Mount Moriah while the sky was dim.
They took wood, the fire, some rope, a knife,
but they forgot to take the ram.
This worries me. I have been the wife
of Abraham for many years, but I am
not as trusting of him as my son.
They did not take a sheep.
Isaac is young. He trusts everyone.
How could he know his father does not sleep
at night but wakes up shaking as he prays,
angels in his head, fire in his gaze?

Five Years
    After Paul Celan

Oak tree, moss drips from your bent limbs.
My son's arms were strong.

Autumn hills, you burn with a cold light.
My son embraces no sister, no mother.

Lake, do you ripple with fish or tears?
My only son swims to the opposite shore.

Fingernail moon, you hang by a dark thread.
My gentle son speaks to me in dreams.

Floor, where is the chair I hurled against you?
My son has a splinter in his heart.

Angeline

She is not an ordinary
Baby but a lump of coal.
Grown-ups glance at her
And look away. Only the children
Stare. Their parents tell them
Not to point.

When Angeline's mother
Wheels her stroller
Into the bakery
Everyone falls silent.
When she pushes it
Outside again, raindrops slide
Right off her baby's face.

At night Angeline's mother
Polishes her daughter's
Lustrous skin, then lugs her up
To her bed of gravel, neatly raked
To resemble a trout stream.

She tells her child the story
Of where she came from,
How the trees rose and fell
Like dynasties, first to swamps
Then to the sea.

When Angeline's mother kisses
Her baby good night, she says,
Sweet dreams, Angeline.
When she turns out the light
Moonlight shatters
Against her daughter's brow.

Running Away

She can't stand
The way her mother slams the door,
The squawk of her mother's voice, stones

Flying from her throat. She will show her.
Look: She opens her bedroom door
Like the lid of a box. Listen to it drag

Across the carpet, the insistent sweep
Of her corduroy slacks as she creeps
Down the hallway, quiet as a broom.

See her hand reach the brass knob,
Pull the front door open, morning sun
Shattering the holly-berry bushes. Monarchs

Flock above the brick walk, mocking her
With rapid wings. Watch the girl go out
Without a sandwich, without her braces

Her crutches, without her ugly chair. She hates
All of them as she hits the black asphalt
On her hands and knees, running away.

From the 22nd Floor

I feel my daughter climbing, bare skin
pressed against the wall. She is scaling
the building one ledge at a time—exhaling,
inhaling—She is desperate to get in.

She climbs up stone and glass as I sit
in my office, facing the window, eyes
half closed, half hoping she'll descend or rise
alone—half knowing she won't make it.

So I forget that I can't save her—slide
back the sash, reach through without a sound,
grab her wrist, the knot of bone inside.
Her hand clamps down and we are wound
into a chain, a sheet that will not tear.
Easy now, I pull her in—She is made of air.

El Norte

When border police lift children from
their mothers' arms, their fathers' hands—
lock them up in cages from El Paso
to El Monte—tossing silver sheets
across small bodies, toddlers cry so hard
they can hardly catch their breath.
Meanwhile agents shuttle parents
onto airplanes like so much cargo,
shipping them to jail in Topeka, Chicago,
after they had walked for weeks
with feet on fire toward El Norte—
the land that was supposed to save them.

When a deported Guatemalan mother
hides her head in her hands, afraid
she will never see her only child again—
Graciela, age seven, who had just learned
to play Mozart on her three-quarter-size violin—
I wonder how my grandparents felt
as they rushed to escape the Czar's army,
descending by nightfall into the cavernous
belly of a ship, tossing for days
on unknown waters. How did it feel
to step off the boat at Ellis Island?
Did Grandpa hoist little Aunt Fanny
to his shoulders, so she could see
the lady holding her lamp high?
Did tears arise in Grandma's eyes,
her belly big with Aunt Sophia,
the one who would become a violinist?

When the US attorney general poses
before TV cameras, smirking as he spouts
chapter and verse to justify ripping
families apart, I think of Thailand
where twelve soccer players—boys
who had never learned to swim—
huddle together deep inside a cave
accessible only by serpentine tunnels, now
flooded. Their coach, a Buddhist monk,
teaches them to meditate so
they can endure the wait.
Meanwhile divers in wetsuits gear up
with scuba tanks and masks—two men
for each boy: one to cradle a child beneath
his body, the other to follow a guide rope
through the tunnel. We follow them
each morning in the news until two by two,
then four, then eight—all the boys,
their coach and guides, are borne
by unseen hands into silver sheets of light.

In a Strange Land
San Miguel de Allende, Mexico, September 14, 2001

It must feel strange, you wrote, to be
in a foreign country at a time like this.
Strange, yes, to walk out of
a two-hundred-year-old building
to the slanting light, strange as that skinny dog
drinking from a courtyard fountain, as the pigeon
on Ignacio Allende's upraised sword.
Strange to notice beauty anywhere—
to see red, white, and green flags waving,
crowds of people shouting *¡Viva La Libertad!*
while all the church bells ring.
Strange to watch fireworks burst
from hissing towers, twirling rings of fire
ascending toward the steeples.
Strange to approach the entrance
to a church, hoping for a vigil
where the kind priest in his bright raiment
might invite us to speak the names
of friends and family in New York City
and then to pray with expats and tourists.
Strange to climb the stairs to another
gorgeous sunset, to a shawl of rain
draped across a distant mountain.
Strange to perceive a jet trail as a flaming
arrow, to hear mariachis from a nearby hotel
playing their impossibly sad violins.

Pandemic Dog Walk

The white-haired woman walked her sandy dog up the steep sidewalk lined with tall, skinny palms. Dog walks were still allowed, so she headed uphill to see the ocean, but the viewpoint was farther away than she had remembered, so she sat down to rest on a weathered wooden bench. Her dog jumped up beside her. The woman gazed at the splendid blue sky and felt grateful to have such a good dog. It was windy, and small wispy clouds drifted swiftly above the tousled trees. Palm fronds whipped around, sounding all the world like metal brushes stroking snare drums. The woman listened for a while. She heard the coo of a mourning dove. Then she stood up, dog leash in hand, and began walking downhill. There were very few people out, some with dogs, some without. When other walkers saw the woman and her dog, they nodded, waved, and stepped into the street. Six feet apart was the rule. The woman waved back, playing her part in the impromptu choreography of kindness. She glanced at the clouds again and felt terribly sad. They looked so innocent as they sailed above the trees in their own blue sea. Clouds had always been her familiar companions no matter where she roamed, making her feel at home in the world. But they knew nothing of this sudden otherworldliness. The dog paid no attention the clouds. She was too busy sniffing the alluring aroma of other dogs, the watermelon fragrance of crushed grass. Maybe, the woman mused, as she and her dog reached their front gate, maybe they would see the ocean another day.

Tranquil Weather

Today, they say, the weather will be tranquil,
serene, peaceful, and still. Only clear skies
and calm breezes will prevail.
No torrential rain, not even a drizzle,
no hurricanes, blizzards, thunder, or hail.
No one will be stalking you today, no footsteps
in the night, no fear. No worries for the child at sea,
the son in the desert with a gun,
the daughter on the streets, your mother
so far away. No desire for the baby
you never had, the job you didn't get.
No longing to forget
what you did wrong or the wrong
that was done to you. No guilt or pain
for what you couldn't fix. No collisions,
collapses, or incisions. No sorrow
that it's almost over, no shame
because it didn't work. No yearning
to be lauded, loved, or simply to be held.
No grief for what was lost, no wishing
it was different. No need—
because today, they say, the weather will be tranquil.

Hotel at the End of the World

Everyone you ever loved
is here. There's your first girlfriend
brushing her hair while counting
to a hundred. She's kept it shiny
just for you. She will recognize you
in an instant as you sit reading in the lobby,
not by your appearance, but by the way
you turn the pages of a book
with the thumb of your left hand.

In another room is your first son,
the one who hasn't spoken to you
since you left his mother.
When you open the door, he will run
to embrace you. Later he will tell you
all about China and the ways they have
of repairing the heart.

When you're alone at last
your mother will appear carrying bolts
of silk and talking nonstop about how
polite the waiters are at this hotel,
how beautiful the view,
and her latest cruise to the Aegean. She says
she has to go now. The helicopter's waiting.
But she'll see you shortly—in another
thirty years or so. She'll bring
Swiss chocolates and gold watches
next time, she promises.

ACKNOWLEDGMENTS

Sincere thanks to the editors of the following magazines and anthologies in which these poems or earlier versions of them appeared:

The Antioch Review: "Hotel at the End of the World"
Crania: "Dark Child"
The Devil's Millhopper: "From the 22nd Floor"
El Independiente: "At La Capilla"
Margie: The American Journal of Poetry: "Blue Carnation," "Michelangelo's Last Judgment"
Mosaic: "Not to Meet Beautiful Strangers," "What Some Men Can Do"
New Letters: "Reflections"
Ploughshares: "Angeline," "Milk Glass," "Portrait, Age Seven," "A Walk at Dusk"
South Coast Poetry Journal: "Girl Waiting" (titled "Indian Girl")
Third Coast: "Running Away"

"Blazon" was first published in *Stand-Up Poetry: The Anthology*, edited by Charles Webb (California State University Press, Long Beach, 1994).
"Five Years" was first published in *Grand Passion: The Poets of Los Angeles and Beyond*, edited by Suzanne Lummis and Charles H. Webb (Red Wind Books, 1995).
"Ghazal for My Ancestors" was first published in *Taj Mahal Review*, edited by Santosh Kumar (Cyberwit.net, 2005).
"The Invention of Singing" was first published in *Jewish Women's Literary Annual 7*, edited by Henny Wenkart (National Council of Jewish Women, 2006).
"Sephirot" was first published in *Nice Jewish Girls: Growing Up in America*, edited by Marlene Adler Marks (Plume, 1996).
"Tranquil Weather" was first published in *Emotional Map of Los Angeles*, edited by Keren Taylor (WriteGirl, 2015).
"What Some Men Can Do" was published in *Last Call: The Bukowski Legacy Continues*, edited by RD Armstrong (Lummox Press, 2020).

Grateful acknowledgment is extended to the California Arts Council for an individual fellowship in poetry; to the J. Paul Getty Trust for a study and renewal leave in San Miguel de Allende, Mexico; to the Warren Wilson MFA Program for Writers and its community of alumni; to the City of Santa Monica, Cultural Affairs for a writer's residency at the Annenberg Community Beach House; and to Shanna McNair and Scott Wolven of The Writer's Hotel for their valuable insights.

Dinah Berland has a background in art and formerly worked as senior editor at Getty Publications in Los Angeles. Her first chapbook, *Fugue for a New Life* (2020), was the 2019 winner of the WaterSedge Poetry Chapbook Contest. She received an individual fellowship in poetry from the California Arts Council, an international prize from the *Atlanta Review*, and was twice nominated for a Pushcart Prize. Her poems have appeared in the *The Antioch Review, The Iowa Review, New Letters, Ploughshares,* and *Third Coast,* among other journals, and are published in many anthologies. Her book *Hours of Devotion: Fanny Neuda's Book of Prayers for Jewish Women* (Schocken Books, 2007) is a verse translation from the German of the first full-length book of prayers by a Jewish woman for women. She earned her MFA in poetry from the Program for Writers at Warren Wilson College and was the spring 2017 Writer in Residence at the Annenberg Community Beach House in Santa Monica. She currently leads the Poetry Oasis workshop from her home in Los Angeles.

www.ingramcontent.com/pod-product-compliance
Lightning Source LLC
LaVergne TN
LVHW041555070426
835507LV00011B/1092